# Foreword

This <u>Ease Your Depression with Gratitude</u> will help you grow and has the potential to change your life.

We highly recommend you begin by completing your list at least once a day.  At the very least, enter two or three things each day for which you are grateful.

It is not necessary to feel like you need to write  down a whole list of items. To begin with, just listing two or three items will start the process.

We believe as you continue to list those things you have gratitude for in your life aright now, you will create a mindset which will encourage the universe to increase the blessings in your life .

You will find as you continue this practice, you will find more and more items for which you are grateful and your outlook on life will improve and you will find your depression eased.

As you continue to "Count Your Blessings" daily. you will see your blessings multiply and your gratitude list expand.

Thank you for your purchase.

# Today I am grateful for...

# Today I am grateful for...

# Today I am grateful for...

# Today I am grateful for…

# Today I am grateful for...

# Today I am grateful for...

# Today I am grateful for...

# Today I am grateful for...

# Today I am grateful for...

# Today I am grateful for...

# Today I am grateful for...

# Today I am grateful for...

# Today I am grateful for...

# Today I am grateful for...

# Today I am grateful for...

# Today I am grateful for…

# Today I am grateful for...

# Today I am grateful for...

# Today I am grateful for...

# Today I am grateful for...

# Today I am grateful for...

# Today I am grateful for...

# Today I am grateful for...

# Today I am grateful for...

# Today I am grateful for...

# Today I am grateful for...

# Today I am grateful for...

# Today I am grateful for...

# Today I am grateful for...

# Today I am grateful for...

# Today I am grateful for...

# Today I am grateful for...

# Today I am grateful for...

# Today I am grateful for...

# Today I am grateful for...

# Today I am grateful for...

# Today I am grateful for...

# Today I am grateful for...

# Today I am grateful for...

# Today I am grateful for...

# Today I am grateful for...

# Today I am grateful for...

# Today I am grateful for...

# Today I am grateful for...

# Today I am grateful for...

# Today I am grateful for...

# Today I am grateful for…

# Today I am grateful for...

# Today I am grateful for...

# Today I am grateful for...

# Today I am grateful for...

# Today I am grateful for...

# Today I am grateful for...

# Today I am grateful for...

# Today I am grateful for...

# Today I am grateful for...

# Today I am grateful for...

# Today I am grateful for...

# Today I am grateful for...

# Today I am grateful for...

# Today I am grateful for…

# Today I am grateful for...

# Today I am grateful for...

# Today I am grateful for...

# Today I am grateful for...

# Today I am grateful for...

# Today I am grateful for…

# Today I am grateful for...

# Today I am grateful for...

# Today I am grateful for...

# Today I am grateful for...

# Today I am grateful for...

# Today I am grateful for…

# Today I am grateful for...

# Today I am grateful for...

# Today I am grateful for...

# Today I am grateful for...

# Today I am grateful for...

# Today I am grateful for...

# Today I am grateful for...

# Today I am grateful for...

# Today I am grateful for...

# Today I am grateful for...

# Today I am grateful for...

# Today I am grateful for...

# Today I am grateful for...

# Today I am grateful for...

# Today I am grateful for...

# Today I am grateful for...

# Today I am grateful for...

# Today I am grateful for...

# Today I am grateful for…

# Today I am grateful for...

# Today I am grateful for...

# Today I am grateful for...

# Today I am grateful for...

# Today I am grateful for...

# Today I am grateful for...

# Today I am grateful for...

# Today I am grateful for...

# Today I am grateful for...

# Today I am grateful for...

# Today I am grateful for...

# Today I am grateful for...

# Today I am grateful for...

# Today I am grateful for...

# Today I am grateful for...

# Today I am grateful for...

# Today I am grateful for...

# Today I am grateful for...

# Today I am grateful for...

# Today I am grateful for...

# Today I am grateful for...

# Today I am grateful for...

# Today I am grateful for...

# Today I am grateful for...

# Today I am grateful for...

# Today I am grateful for...

# Today I am grateful for...

# Today I am grateful for...

# Today I am grateful for...

## About Front Porch Press

Front Porch Press Is a small publisher located in Bulverde, Texas, often called "The Front Porch" of the Texas hill country.

We have published other helpful journals and planners and also digital  stories available on Amazon Kindle, Barnes and Noble Nook, Kobo, and other digital retailers.